First, Then

WOLFE JESSIE

BookLeaf
Publishing

India | USA | UK

Presentation by *BookLeaf Publishing*

Web: www.bookleafpub.com

E-mail: info@bookleafpub.com

ISBN: 9789357446556

First edition 2022

DEDICATION

For Rory, Claire, Shannon, Jayden,
Melanie, Jack, Kate, Jax and Sinead.

ACKNOWLEDGEMENT

With deepest gratitude to old lovers, and dear friends, deep connections and brief romances. To severed ties and heartache, late nights and growing pains. To the hands that held and nurtured. To those from before, those that have always been there, and those who are there now.

Without which, no feelings would be felt, no lessons learned, and these words would not be here.

And now to you,
Your hands on these pages, your eyes on these words -

Thank you.

First, This

Rocks stacked
Snakes writhing around each other
Like DNA ribbons
Hands clenched into fists
A ceramic vessel, heart shaped,
Cracked in two
Fingertips reaching toward one another and the
distance in-between
Your hands
Your bed
Knife edge

A Taste of The End

Pain and power
I eat it up like raspberries and my insides
                    Rot
Tell me a story
        of love that filled you up

With   warmth
                            wonder
                    wildflowers

Backwards

You tie your shoelaces backwards.
Trigger the domino effect without consequence.
You've been wearing the same shoe size for
years, but you're still growing into them.
Shenanigans. Always silly buggers and bottle
caps. Throwing fruit for flies and birds to feast
on.
You're running barefoot and waist deep through
a grass field on a dewey winter morning at dawn
and you don't know why.
You're yelling in your sleep again.
There's a man at the end of your bed.
He's got claws and teeth! You said.
You're looking in the mirror when you say this.
You're not you. Words and sharp teeth and
shadows. Sharper sentences caress soft necks.
Another bird dies somewhere.
The nectarines are rotting and there are no flies
in sight. There will be no feasting. The crows
gather around their dead.
We only see things when they've passed, you
know.
Everything is backwards in the end.

Words of Warmth and Wisdom.

Things are changing, always changing, ever evolving - a constant state of motion. Like being stuck inside a revolving door. I don't want to be a mouse on a wheel. If I'm running, it's toward something, more real, more tangible, a full bodied experience. Some days, my body halts, suddenly, and my hip joints feel rusty. Betrayed by my insides, agony, forced to move slowly, to be softer, to give more love to myself, less to the ether. I'm okay with the slower pace, mostly. I'll fold myself into square shapes and think more of love and heartache, the way things change, the love we save, or don't, for ourselves.

All and Sundry, With Ears to See

Salt in the wound, only in it for the game -

Men like you

Drowning in self obsessed selfishness

Puppet-master and his strings.

Vile, vulgar, and volatile.

Just another bottle, another body to break the
spell -
another mouth to crawl inside of.

Another skinhead with booze breath and greedy
hands.

Ephialtes on your chest in the darkness.

Another girl caught the web.

Pain and power

You eat it up like raspberries and your insides
                    Rot
Tell me a story
            of love that filled you up

With   warmth
                              wonder
                  wildflowers

You can't.

The Coffin That Sand Built

Peaches and bird wings,
Berries and ruffled feathers
Lavender in the breast pocket of the oversized
button down shirt
Muddled mind, dappled light, daydreaming of
wax dripping and
Silence
Down down down the rabbit hole
Into the hourglass, built a coffin out of sand
Built a home in your hands
You, the girl in silk black as night
The girl in the bell jar with the bones and wilted
petals and
Words
About the bump in the night
Skeletons in the closet tap tap tapping from the
inside
Motion picture behind eyes
Watching
Sandalwood and citrus peel
Claw foot bathtub to sink into

Melting
Melting
Melting

The First Encounter

In a room full of people
You put your arms around me,
like an old friend
and my skin
crawls
at your touch -
My body is a suit of armour screaming
that's enough that's enough.
No sincerity, no real words, no sorry.
Reality shifts like gravel under the soles of my
feet and my stomach flips.
You are a stranger, with your hands on my skin.
Leave. Do not look at me.
Do not greet me with a warm smile, and open
arms.
We are not old friends.

Coping Mechanism

Trembling fingers, hands holding sneakers.
Butterflies and belly flips, hesitation forgone -
lace them swiftly. Two delicate flowers growing
lonely in a garden bed of weeds where this street
meets the next. The very same blue. Air crisp
and salt scented, sun - keeping the balance. Blue
Sunday to the beat of feet falling on the
pavement. Hell for leather up Parkway Ave, sky
kissing water in the distance. A divine display,
infinite, all consuming, teasing. Some place
other, another body in another pair of sneakers
leaps gracefully over the railing and runs full
speed across the ever moving surface. Pipe
dream. This body follows the white wood posts
along the coastline. Cognisance wrestles with
old habits.

At Twenty Three

I made my way into the belly of the beast, and
emerged anew. A new woman,
A new soul
A new soulful dance between body and vessel
Entwined, tangled, swallowed whole
Heart brimming with the fierce and fiery passion
of a love reborn
Swimming with the soft and soft and sombre
solace of a gentle tender touch
Fingertips trembling
Wanting
Waiting, yearning
Deep down, a flame ignited
A passion brewing, growing, burning.

Reverie's Castle Is A Body Dressed In Diamonds

1

Warm smiles and bodies in bedsheets - pretend you're in love, for a while. Brush teeth stood beside each other, pulling silly faces in the mirror. Leave the future at the door where the shoes are, and the details on the table, by the glass of water on the bedside. Breathe the same air more often, hide poetic verse and sweet words on paper tucked beneath pillowcases and and in coat pockets, to find on rainy days. Clumsily spill red wine on that favourite white shirt and fall into fits of laughter. Let the stain soak in, a memory - of the photos not taken, the letters not written. Soft kisses on closed eyelids in the late mornings. Shared breakfasts and cold leftovers and sweet words, sweet nothings. Desire drips from warm bodies with the steady

heartbeat rhythm of the tap leaking water in the
bathroom.

2

Hazy spring sunrise together, two bodies tangled
in the water, trying to keep warm. Pre-made
stovetop coffee between soft fingertips. Legs
tremble as mouths meet. More than deep belly
laughter. More than the last desperate steps feet
take to the place at the hills top where streets
meet. If you were, for a day, the person you
always dreamed of being, who would you be?
Does your body tremble too? Does the dark
scare and encompass you? Pretend you're in
love with me. Sulfur and charcoal and saltpetre
meet with fire in the same way the sky's
particulate matter seems to scatter at dawn.
Slowly, then all at once. The same way I
crumble, in your presence. The way globes
warm to brightness when you click the switch.
Pretend, we've never met. Let's start again. We
are just two bodies watching the sun inch his
gaze toward a new day. You'll smile, I'll ask
your name.

Empty Womb

Turmeric and honey in warm milk, doesn't ease the pain, but I pretend it will - my pelvic floor feels full, of barbed wire and razor blades, and I think of how I bled, for thirteen days; the body's taunting, a visceral display, a new kind of mourning. Guilt cuddles up to relief, and we have a pity party on a drop sheet, in the living room. There's a dull echo in my womb. But in these walls, floor cushions and hands to hold while tears and truth meld tight together and intertwine. Word sounds that must be mine, transparency that took time, to surface - to come to terms with. Reflection, foreign, moving, missing. Sweet souls listening, comforting. Turmeric and honey, a slow but steady heartbeat, love in abundance.

Fervour Dream

Oh to
Dance with you
Feel our bodies move,
Same time same place same room
Maybe steal a glance or two
Pleasure senses, keeping distance
Salt dew drops shining like stars on the skins
surface
There's
A magnetism, to your presence
Effervescent coexistence
Mind lingers on the space between the place that
the jawline meets the base
Of your neck
Hands hover, mid air, amidst movement,
reaching
Daydreams and desire, fuel enough, to feel the
rush
A quiet admiration

Maybe Pain is a Piece of Glass

Dazed and dusty. Teetering on the edge of delirium and insanity. Pain moves through me, thudding to each heart beat with the eerie, menacing rumbling of a kick drum, and I lean into it, because, what else. Hell on earth Is a place inside my skin suit, body failing, betraying. A cycle, unpredictable - unfamiliar hands invade and poke and prod and answers only pave a road to additional questions and less certainty. My body is a stand up comedy gig running overtime and I am an unsettled audience uncomfortably awaiting the punchline. Inconclusive? You're kidding right. I'm tired, aren't you tired? The girl in the mirror doesn't answer. Maybe I'm dreaming, maybe hell is a hallucination, maybe pain is just a piece of glass. Maybe, if I scream loud enough, I can shatter the illusion. I get the joke now, can you see me laughing? I'm ready to wake up.

Purgatory Body

The sun rises and falls
Like my chest with each breath and
Time is slipping away -
Hands curled into fists, nails in palms, split
flesh, blood drips.
Is it light or dark that you like less?
Where do you hold your darkness?
Does it weigh your body down?
Pensive thoughts -
Intrusive.
Crisp air strips me bare and slices me open,
insides exposed.
Stitches come undone, no will to run, too tired to
try anyway.
The memories buried in places unseen let loose,
float to the surface.
Lights out, submerged in the darkness. No spark
in the distance. Letters of words on pain and loss
rolled up and cork sealed in bottles.
Hands shake, the crate drops.
Glass shards swarm like wasps, embed like
splinters, in my consciousness.
My darkness? It's in my blood, pumping through
my body with each heartbeat, cyclical.
Immersed again, reliving.

My mind leaves my body to watch from a
distance.
A safer place to rest.

The Unlearning

He is porcelain, beauty in a way I thought I
could never quantify, never grasp, never
understand
Never feel beneath my hands
I've got a history, of only laying with men who
leave me bruised - in one way, or another
Sometimes on the skin for eyes to see, but
beneath it, predominantly
Left tender where the heart beats
I don't know how to be vulnerable to kindness
To be seen by eyes that don't press and pressure
Don't know how
To give in when it's an option and not a given
I'm shaken
By compassion, in the bedroom
What a sad thing, to come to terms with
But a blessing;
To be stronger, to feel worth it.

Fruit For Thought

I bet you smell like ground coffee beans and
citrus, picking apart the mandarin piece by piece
with slender paint covered fingertips.
I split mine in two, peel holding each half like an
offering, cupped in both hands.
One summer afternoon, my uncle patiently
peeled thirteen oranges, in silence, with a pocket
knife. I wanted to know how he carved the skin
into perfect spirals, how his work weathered old
hands moved the blade between flesh and skin
so delicately. Swift precision, no blood on the
tabletop.
That summer I collected fruit seeds in my
pockets, sun dried them on the windows ledge,
dreamed of a citrus tree tall enough to climb up
up and get lost in. Head in the clouds.
Kaleidoscope of green and orange, blue sky and
dappled sunlight. A perfect place to hide.
I was too young to know love, then. Too naïve,
to know practice, patience. Not yet hardened by
hardship - still learning to be still.
On this warm mid morning, I hold the fruit in
each palm and dream of being still beneath the
leaves instead. Blades of grass gently blowing in
the breeze, surrounding me. A quiet place to sit,

to hold out my hand, offer you half, to hear you laugh. For there is joy enough in solitude, it's true. But nothing quite compares to marvelling at magic beside another body with a heartbeat. To taste the nectar on your lips. A unique and disparate bliss.

Ninth Circle

Awake
But not quite, the eyes but a lens to the
subconscious. Three-thirty three post meridem
light
       dances, body stirrs.
It's warm here.
It's all wrong, here. All the pieces come together
jumbled up like soup letters.
Alphabet soup, whatever.
For   the   briefest
       moment,
I was dozing peacefully,
Sun caressed on a secondhand mattress on the
third floor
of the church house
         on the hill
I come to sun caressed on my own bed
Little red house, little breath left
It's all sunlight and static until it isn't
Jagged glass shards in my chest all over again
         you left.
And for a moment, just a moment I didn't know
that quite yet
It all comes back at once.

White noise and then silence
It's been eight
Months
Of you in my dreams
Eight nights at the altar on my knees
Praying to the gods
                 take him
Burn what's left in me
The gods laugh and take me instead into the
depths, left
Somewhere between heresy and treachery
Just   bury me
In the ninth circle frozen beneath the bodies of
the deceased
I'd rather be
Asleep

The Incline

I would have let it kill me
Bare body kneeling in glass letting the shards
sink in and split skin
Begging
My body on the pavement, belly up
Eyes wide looking to the sky the sun still shines
and birds fly
but my
Heart stopped on church street,
Soul torn
and I've been drawing dead birds and spilling
words into verse and onto pages
So many yarns spun webs weaved
Too many echo's
in this
place.
Funeral for my old self
The girl who begged.
Flames lick photographs and melt memories and
they crumble to ash like magic,
The snake sheds her layers and awaits claw tips
to tear through flesh spread wings
Become the dragon

Aftermath: Ongoing

Some days, I'm peeling potatoes in my kitchen and it's 2018 and we're in our apartment. It was always Johnny Cash with you, beer in hand, windows open, sundown view. You're flicking a cigarette butt off the balcony again.

I tear the stitches out in my sleep. It's 2021 and I don't remember how we got here. I'm peeling mandarin's in the bathtub. I dyed my hair blue. I'm not her, anymore.

I had to quit tobacco. The smell on my fingertips in the mornings kept reminding me of you. But I can't quit myself and you're still under my skin in splinters and fragments. I'm bleeding on the potatoes. I still remember what your voice sounds like. I'm not her anymore.

I slice myself open for you one last time. I've said that before. This time, I burn your photographs, one by one. Full moons light, small fire in the backyard. The snake grew wings, I guess. Armour made of scales and claws and teeth. I read it takes six months for a fingernail to grow back. Sometimes love is a candle, sometimes love is just a matchstick, splinters in my skin. That doesn't even mean anything. I'm

just saying words. You were just saying words,
in the end. Liars Labyrinth.

Rose Coloured Echo

The memory of you
Reverberates,
Dances around the inside of my cranium
The way fingertips tip toe atop keys -
Fleeting fragments,
Stretched out standstills, passing slowly through
My mind, racing
To hold on to transience
Trembling to touch,
Nerve endings subsuming each caress
Heart palpitating to the beat of bodies
Perfervid, passional, in motion
Pockets in time
Left behind
Still somewhere, still burning
Blissful
Blazing, a fire indoors,
A crisp and inclement period
Between sunrise
And sunset

Parallels and Synchronicities

222
Two taps on the wall
Two footsteps in the hall
Two friends that I'll call
To ease the tension
Tell tale heart beating in the dark hours.

3:33
Witching hour
Two bodies in my dream,
reaching.
Always at a crossroads.
Summoning circle,
sold my soul to the devil
In exchange for a jar of time.
Weeping amber tears,
pocket full of sand,
clock ticking without
hands.

The Final Resting

I'm surprised,
At the peace, and quiet, in my mind
My body, softens easily, and sleep holds me
silently in its arms, most nights
There was a darkness to us, in the end
Like two people wedged between book ends and
dull dusty hardcovers, on an old wooden shelf,
with the lights off
Love long forgotten, left with just the echo of
what once was.
And just like that
None of it matters anymore
Somewhere my self trades grief and pain for
silence. No misery, no joy no hopelessness. The
sun casts shadows on the window sill and the pin
pricks in the skin on my body's left side sting a
little. But nothing feels like much of anything. It
just.. is. I become a silent observer, seeing
beauty but feeling nothing. Nothing and
everything, everything and nothing. A full circle.
Stillness and solitude, a time of waiting, the grey
area. A place to rest a while.